To: _____

From: _____

Date: _____

Cat Confessions

A "KITTY COME CLEAN" TELL-ALL BOOK

By Allia Zobel Nolan

HARVEST HOUSE PUBLISHERS

EUGENE, OREGON

Cat Confessions

Text Copyright © 2010 by Allia Zobel Nolan

Photos compiled by Allia Zobel Nolan
Except where otherwise noted, all photos: Shutterstock
Photos on pages 21 and 27 copyright © 2009 Bernadette E.
Kazmarski, used by permission
Pages 54 and 58 BigStockPhoto

Published by Harvest House Publishers
Eugene, Oregon 97402
www.harvesthousepublishers.com

ISBN: 978-0-7369-2711-6

Design and production by Mary pat Design, Westport, Connecticut

www.AlliaWrites.com

Printed in China
17 18 19 20 / LP / 21 20 19 18

For God, my sincere thanks for making me a cat person, not a dog person; for my husband, Desmond, who puts up with the puddies but would really rather have a springer spaniel; and for my three furry children: my eldest, Angela Dah-ling, who'd never do anything untoward (while I was watching), MacDuff, my 23-pounder, who gets into more trouble than I can elaborate here because of space, and Sineady-Cat-the-Fraidy-Cat, my shy black and white beauty, who never meows except when Daddy wants to sleep in.

–Allia Zobel Nolan

Buy this now, or it's bargain kitty litter for every cat in this book. I hate bargain kitty litter.

🐾 Persuasive Puddy
Eugene, Oregon

A Short Paws to Reflect

While I'm loath to admit it, I have heard rumors among some cat people that their itty-bitty, wide-eyed, Mommy's-darling puddies can at times be, well, naughty.

Having lived with cats all my life, I know they're very sensitive beings, and as such I came to the conclusion that the kitties who fall into this category may just feel the need to own up to their inequities, get things off their chests, and confess to an incident, bad habit, or hidden secret that could possibly damage the special bond they share with other creatures, be they two- or four-legged.

Then, too, we all know how tremendously cat-hartic the act of coming clean can be. Indeed, and that's what this book is all about—a means for those fallen-away furry angels to admit their mistakes, start afresh, and change their lives (all nine of them) forever, so they can hold their whiskers high and be an example to all who would follow in their pawsteps.

It takes a lot of guts to make these admissions. And I applaud each and every puddie who consented to be a part of this communal cleansing. Bravo!

My cats? No, you won't get the skinny on them here because, in my book, they can do no wrong (or at least if they do wrong, they'll never own up to it).

–Allia Zobel Nolan

All we did was tell Mommy's date how old she *really* is. We don't know why he left.

Sugar & Spice
Duluth,
Minnesota

There were these aliens, see, with heads like flutes and five huge mouths, and they flew into the kitchen and ate up all Mommy's shrimp. Then they turned and chased me into the garden here. Why, I barely escaped with my life!

🐾 Flash, Kansas City, Kansas

Okay, I prefer *sitting* on couches rather than *shredding* them. That's okay, isn't it?

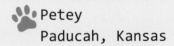

Petey
Paducah, Kansas

I bought him in
the Hamptons...
at a yard sale.
I couldn't help
myself.

 Socks
Darien,
Connecticut

13

So I was minding my own business, staring at a bug, when this gigantic hairball shot out of my mouth, like a cannonball and—*SMACK*—landed right in Daddy's shoe. I mean, I couldn't do it again if I tried.

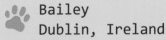

Bailey
Dublin, Ireland

We lick the salt off the potato chips when Mommy has company.

Ham, Shem, and Japheth
Nashville, Tennessee

It was in my email. See, this cat king was like deposed from his country, and he had ten million salmon in a cold vault. And if I gave him Mommy's credit card number, he could pay the tax, get the fish out, and sell them for a gazillion dollars. Mom's investment would quadruple. I thought she'd be proud of me.

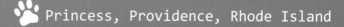 Princess, Providence, Rhode Island

19

We're not allowed to use the computer. But when Daddy leaves it on... Well... Hey, Kyler, is that your new fan page? Kewl!

Kyler and Cassidy
Cambridge, Massachusetts

Flowers? Well, yeah,
I ate them. They were
mine, weren't they?
I thought everything
was mine. Isn't it?

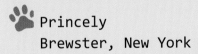 Princely
    Brewster, New York

22

Okay, so I introduced my compadre, Coyote, to Pablocito, the neighbor's Chihuahua. What? Did I do something wrong?

Freddy
Redding, Connecticut

When Mom's on vacation,
we invite our friends for
pool parties in the tub.
But we lick it clean when
we're through.

Mewsette and Jelly Bean
Pittsburgh, Pennsylvania

Me? Jealous? Why, I'm way cuter than that itty-bitty, silly, know-nothing, meowing, attention-seeker Mommy brought home yesterday. Aren't I?

Precious and
What's Her Name
Houston, Texas

Sometimes I help Mom
tenderize the steak.

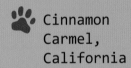 Cinnamon
Carmel,
California

I signed up for an online yoga class. This is my downward dog. Nice, huh? They said the course was free, but then I got a bill...so I ate it.

Ramsey
Denver, Colorado

I'm crashing Mommy's honeymoon. Am I there yet?

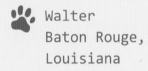 Walter
Baton Rouge,
Louisiana

I sat on Mrs. O'Reilly's
black coat on purpose.

Fluffy
Tipperary,
Ireland

This is more of a brag than a confession—one of my hairballs just made it into the *Guinness World Records*. Is that K-E-W-L, or what?

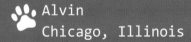

Alvin
Chicago, Illinois

One of us wears dentures.

I used Daddy's razor.

Spock
Miami,
Florida

I only chewed through those wires so Mom would spend less time at the computer and more time petting me.

Willy
Richmond, Virginia

I hate milk! There, I've said it. Now would someone be so kind as to order me a grandé double-mocha cappuccino with two shots of espresso?

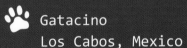 Gatacino
Los Cabos, Mexico

47

I told Dad it was the cleaning lady who dropped his mouse on the floor, but I did it. And I'll do it again if this one doesn't stop staring at me.

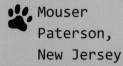 Mouser
Paterson,
New Jersey

49

I like to sneak up behind the cat sitter and hiss when she's watching a scary movie. Boy, can she scream!

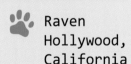

Raven
Hollywood,
California

I've been using Dad's teeth whitening strips. (Sorry, Dad.) Hey, but how do my teeth look? Any brighter? Huh...huh?

Luther
Madison, Wisconsin

We love,
love, love
Mommy. But
her cooking...
Yech!

Jack and Julia
Norwalk,
Connecticut

Sometimes I break things and then pretend to be asleep so Mommy thinks the dog did it.

 Calvin
Atlanta, Georgia

He called me "pretty kitty, pretty kitty" once too often. Sorry I didn't save you any.

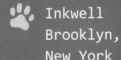 Inkwell
Brooklyn,
New York

Sometimes, when Mommy's out of town, I borrow her red beret for my book club meetings. It makes me feel so literary.

 C.S. Louise
London, England

A confession? Yeah, I have one: My mom's not a cat, and, well, I love her anyway. Is that too weird?

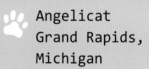

Angelicat
Grand Rapids,
Michigan

When I want extra treats, I hide and wait ten—maybe fifteen—minutes after Mommy calls. When she's sufficiently frantic, I make my appearance. Works every time.

🐾 Sassafras, Columbus, Ohio